GW00467885

Alfred's Basic Piano Library

Piano

Fun Book · Level 2

A COLLECTION OF 19 ENTERTAINING SOLOS

Triangle Pianos
SOUTHAMPTON
023 8055 2656

The pleasure of making music can be greatly enhanced if a variety of solo material is available that is fun to play and is well suited to the abilities of the performer. FUN BOOK 2 provides 19 entertaining pieces graded to fit precisely with Level 2 of Alfred's Basic Piano Library. These selections may be used *in addition to* or *instead of* the pieces in RECITAL BOOK 2, to provide reinforcement of the concepts emphasized in each piece.

This book also answers the often expressed need for a variety of supplementary material for use when two or more students from one family are studying the same course and prefer not to play exactly the same pieces.

The pieces in this book may be used to add interest and amusement to the lesson, as well as to recitals and family performances. Many of the subjects for the selections composed especially for this book were suggested by students and teachers, and it is our hope that this book will live up to its name in every way.

Willard A. Palmer · Morton Manus · Amanda Vick Lethco

A General MIDI disk is available (8571), which includes a full piano recording and background accompaniment.

Third Edition

4.95

2

Entertainment!

Use after ALOUETTE (page 6) or
ODE TO JOY (page 7), LESSON BOOK 2.

C POSITION

Allegro moderato

For the repeat, see footnote! *

mf Mak - ing mu - sic's en - ter - tain - ment,

En - ter - tain - ment, en - ter - tain - ment! Mak - ing mu - sic's

en - ter - tain - ment, Lots of fun for you and me!

1.

2. me!

ritardando- - - - - - - - - - - - - - - -

*With this piece you can have fun doing a special trick!
When you repeat, play the left hand one octave higher, and cross the right hand OVER the left, playing the right
hand one octave lower. This is easy to do after you have learned to play the piece as written, and it has a very
special sound. Be sure the R.H. is *over* the L.H., NOT *under* !

Use after LAVENDER'S BLUE (page 9).

Medley of English Dances

("Shepherd's Hey" & "Call the Guard")

Allegro

"Shepherd's Hey"

Fine

"Call the Guard"
(As written)

D.C. al Fine

4

Happy Holiday

Use after KUM-BA-YAH! (page 11).

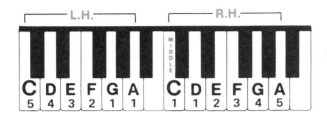

Allegro moderato

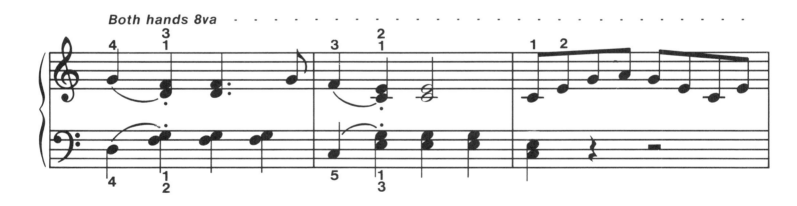

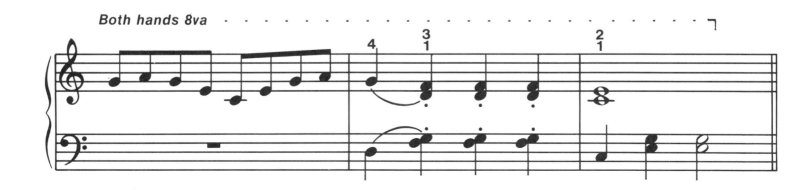

Both hands 2 octaves higher

rit - - ar - - dan - - do - - - - - -

6

I'm Gonna Sing!

Use after 18TH CENTURY DANCE (page 13).

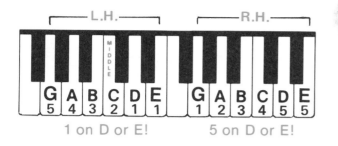

Allegro

Spiritual

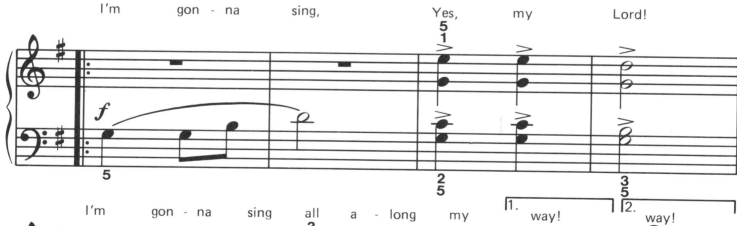

Use after NICK NACK PADDY WACK (page 15).

The Old Gray Mare

Allegro moderato

For the repeat, see footnote!

The old gray mare, she ain't what she used to be,

Ain't what she used to be, ain't what she used to be, The

old gray mare, she ain't what she used to be,

f Man - y long years a - go!

*OPTIONAL: On the repeat, play the left hand as written, but cross the right hand *over* the left hand, and play the R.H. *two octaves lower than written.* This is easy to do after you have learned the piece, and is a very effective trick!

Use after LONE STAR WALTZ (pages 16-17).

Listen to the Mocking Bird

Andante moderato

Alice Hawthorne

2nd time both hands 8va

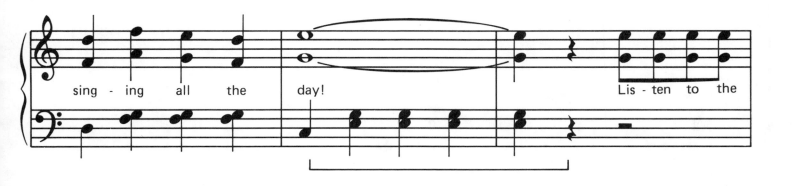

singing all the day!   Lis - ten to the

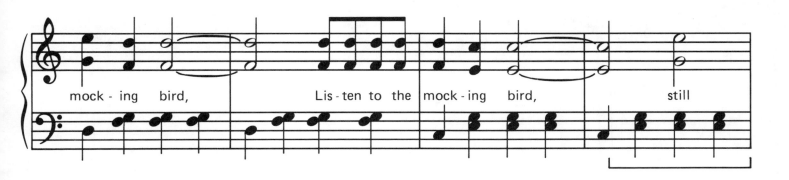

mock - ing bird,   Lis - ten to the mock - ing bird,   still

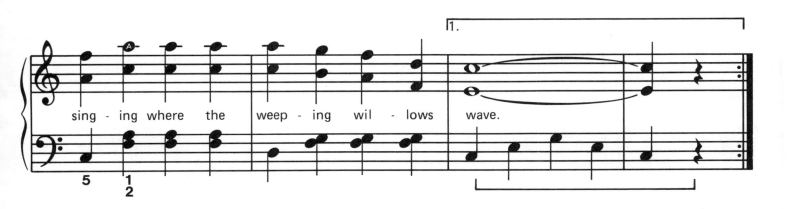

sing - ing where the weep - ing wil - lows wave.

wave.   *rit - - ar - - dan - - do - - - - -*

10

Use after CROSSING R.H. 2 over 1 (page 18).

Be Kind to Your Web-Footed Friends

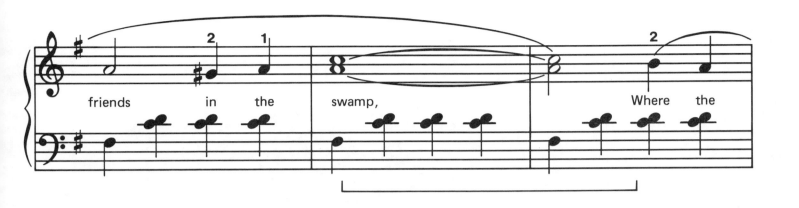

friends in the swamp, Where the

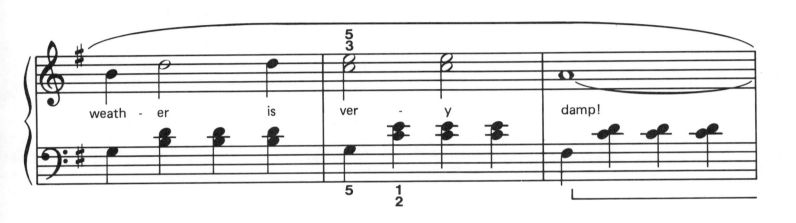

weath - er is ver - y damp!

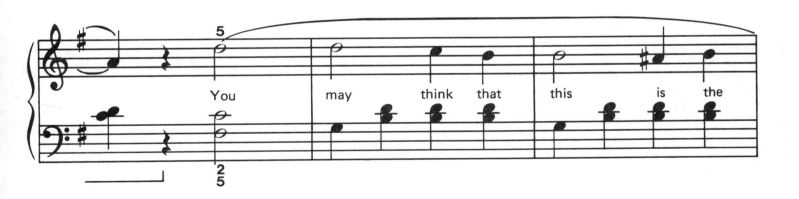

You may think that this is the

end. *f* Well, it is!

12

Ragtime Man

Use after MALAGUEÑA (pages 20–21).

Not fast!

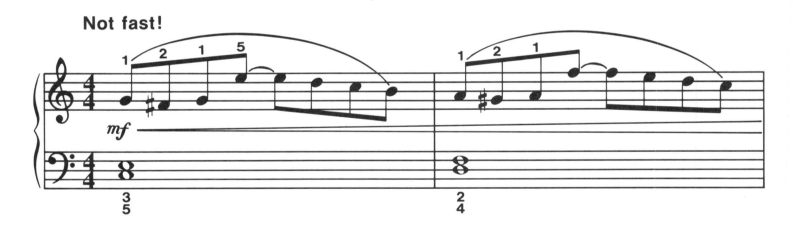

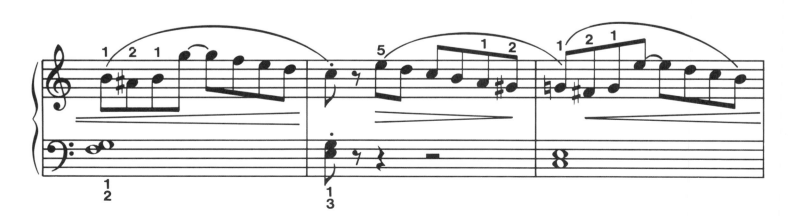

Fine

D.C. al Fine

The Organ Grinder

Use after OUR SPECIAL WALTZ (page 23).

Mexican Serenade

Use after PRELUDE (page 25).

Andante moderato

(Relaxed and quiet)

18

Use after THE CAN-CAN (page 27).

Whistlin' Sam

Andante moderato

*OPTIONAL: All pairs of eighth notes may be played long-short.

Where he goes

No one knows!

Tips a - long,

Slips a - long,

Whist - lin' this old song.

p

(Vanishing away)

pp

20

Use after THE GALWAY PIPER (page 29).

Sounds from Switzerland

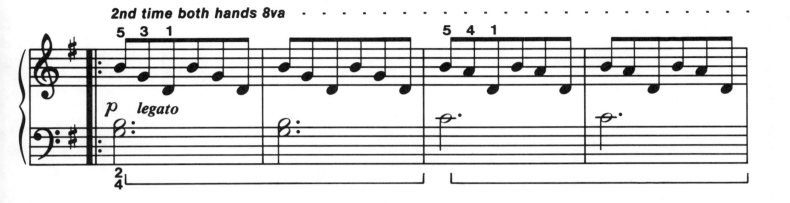

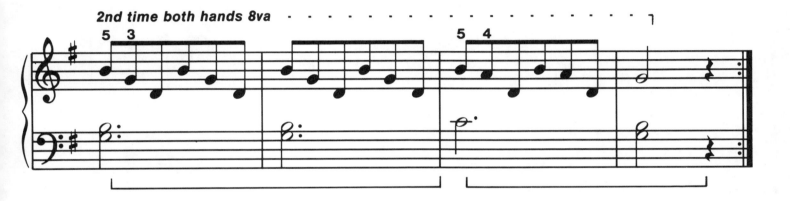

Adagio moderato

The Harmonica Player

Use after COCKLES AND MUSSELS (pages 32-33).

*OPTIONAL: Pedal on each L.H. chord.

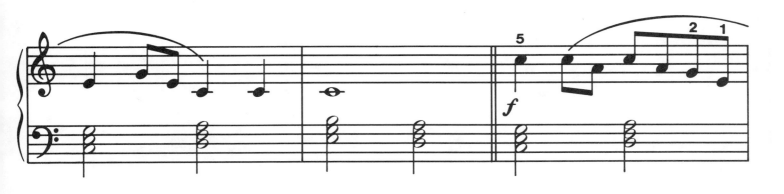

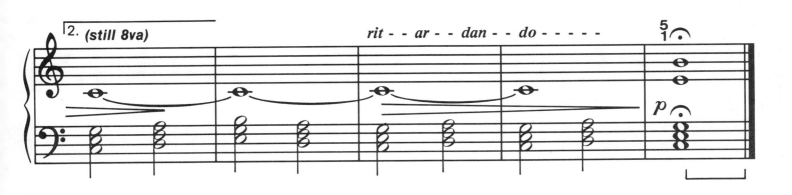

Got Those Blues!

Use after BLUE SCALES (page 35).

Moderato

*The eighth notes may be played a bit unevenly: long   short,   long   short, etc.

Use after GOT LOTSA RHYTHM! (page 37).

The Song That Never Ends!

If you feel that you *must* end this song, do not stop at the last measure! Repeat the first four measures over and over, gradually fading away.

Use after RED RIVER VALLEY (page 40).

Old Country Music

KEY OF G MAJOR
Key Signature: one sharp (F♯)

Andante moderato

mf Old coun - try songs played in old coun - try style;

That's what they want me to play.

Old coun - try songs bring a tear or a smile;

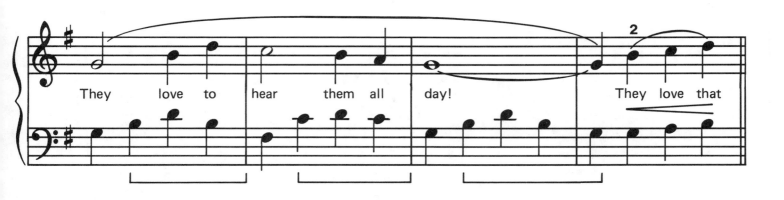

They love to hear them all day! They love that

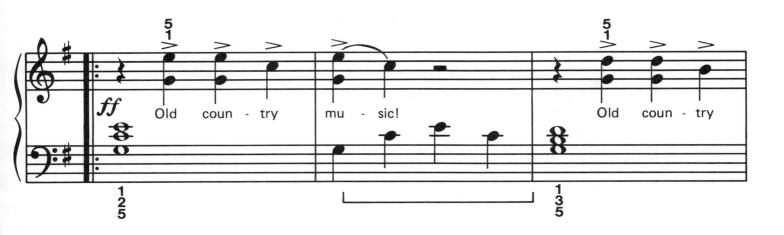

Old coun - try mu - sic! Old coun - try

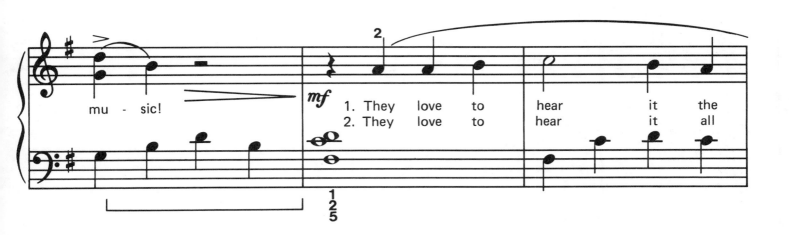

mu - sic! 1. They love to hear it the
2. They love to hear it all

1. whole day long! They love that | 2. day! p

Stroll in the Park

Use after OH SUSANNA! (page 45).

Both hands 8va - - - - - - - - -

pp

Use after SARASPONDA (page 47).

The Cricket and the Bullfrog

This piece reviews the keys of D major, G major and C major.

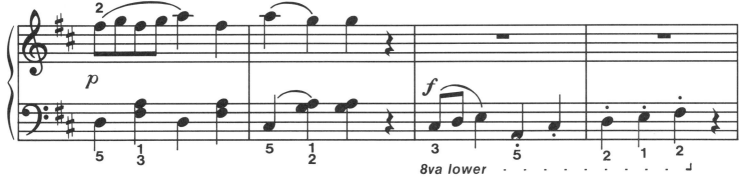

Fine

D.C. al Fine

32

Walkin' the Basses

Use after OH SUSANNA! (page 45) or
SARASPONDA (page 46).

KEY OF D MAJOR
Key Signature: 2 sharps (F♯ & C♯)

Andante

L.H. one octave lower 2nd time

"Two, three, four!" *

* Speak these words loudly when performing.

The rhythm between the two hands may be played "long-short."